THE
CHEYENNE

by Sally Lodge

Illustrated by Luciano Lazzarino

ROURKE PUBLICATIONS, INC.

VERO BEACH, FLORIDA 32964

CONTENTS

Library of Congress Cataloging-in-Publication Data

Lodge, Sally, 1953-
   The Cheyenne / by Sally Lodge.
      p.   cm. —(Native American people)
   Includes index.
   Summary: Presents the history, customs, and present-day status of the Cheyenne Indians.
   1. Cheyenne Indians—Juvenile literature. [1. Cheyenne Indians. 2. Native American People.] I. Title. II. Series.
   E99.C53L63 1990   973′.004973—dc20   90-8476
   ISBN 0-86625-387-4   AC

INTRODUCTION

Originally, the Cheyenne lived in the area just north and west of the Great Lakes. In the late 1600s, the tribe began moving westward across Minnesota and into North Dakota.

When the Cheyenne reached the Missouri River, they built villages on the river banks, where they lived for many years. In small groups, the tribe then migrated further westward. By the early 1800s, many of the Cheyenne had settled in the Black Hills of South Dakota. There the tribes stayed for generations.

The Cheyenne nation is made up of two groups, the Cheyenne and the Suhtai. In the early 1800s, the two were separate tribes, but the Suhtai were gradually absorbed into the Cheyenne. Along with two other tribes, the Arapahoes and the Blackfeet, the Cheyenne belong to a larger Native American family known as the western Algonquians.

Over the years, different stories have emerged to explain how the Cheyenne people were named. According to Cheyenne legend, in early times the tribe called itself *Ni-oh-ma-ate-a-nin-ya*, a long word that means "Desert People." But it was another tribe — the Sioux — that actually gave the Cheyenne its modern name.

The Sioux thought that "Desert People" meant that the Cheyenne were in the habit of painting their faces and bodies with paints made from the red earth. So this tribe gave the Cheyenne a name describing that practice: *Shi-hel-la*. This name evolved into *Shi-hen-na*, which was picked up by the white settlers. The settlers then turned the word into *Cheyenne*.

At the beginning of the nineteenth century, the Cheyenne began a migration that by 1825 had split the tribe into two distinct groups. Some bands of the tribe, looking for a warmer climate and richer hunting grounds, moved into Colorado and settled on the Arkansas River. This group became known as the Southern Cheyenne.

The Cheyenne who remained in the Black Hills became known as the Northern Cheyenne. They gradually moved west into Wyoming and Montana. The two groups remained friendly, and often joined together in battle against common enemies.

Today, the tribe is still divided into two groups. The Southern Cheyenne now live in Oklahoma, and the Northern Cheyenne live in Montana. More than 160 years after the split occurred, the groups are still in close communication, and many Cheyenne travel from one location to the other to visit their relatives.

The history of the Cheyenne is a bittersweet story of dramatic victories and crushing defeats. The Cheyenne way of life changed drastically in the nineteenth century, as the white man's frontier moved westward into the Great Plains. This was the home of the Cheyenne and the other plains tribes, and they refused to give up their land without a fight.

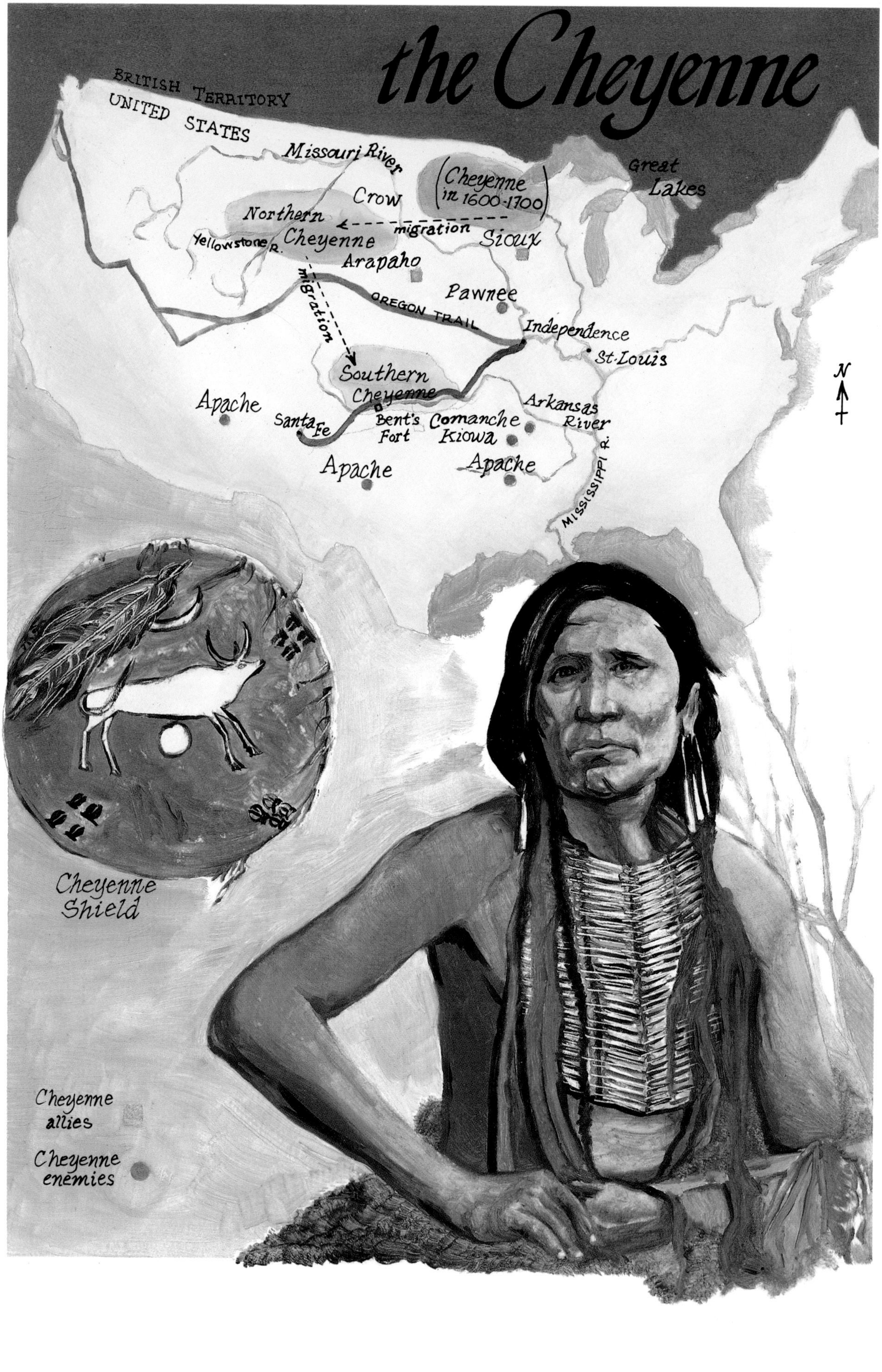

the Cheyenne
BRITISH TERRITORY
UNITED STATES
Missouri River
Cheyenne in 1600-1700
Great Lakes
Crow
Northern Cheyenne
migration
Sioux
Yellowstone R.
Arapaho
Pawnee
OREGON TRAIL
Independence
St. Louis
migration
Southern Cheyenne
Apache
Santa Fe
Bent's Fort
Comanche
Kiowa
Arkansas River
Apache
Apache
MISSISSIPPI R.
N
Cheyenne Shield
Cheyenne allies
Cheyenne enemies

The Early Years

IN THE 1600s and early 1700s, when the Cheyenne lived near the Great Lakes and then built villages on the Missouri River, they were a peaceful tribe. They stayed in one place for long periods of time and did not roam about.

At first, the Cheyenne lived in simple, small huts made of animal skins. As the tribe migrated westward and took up residence on the Great Plains, the Cheyenne built earth-covered tents or lodges. Eventually, these lodges were covered with tanned buffalo skins.

In their settlements on the Missouri River, the Cheyenne were hard-working farmers who grew corn, beans, and squash. They lived off these crops, and also ate wild fruits and roots. For additional food, the men of the tribe hunted birds and small game.

Until the middle of the 1700s, buffalo hunting was only a part-time occupation of the Cheyenne and other farming tribes of the plains. Hunting buffalo was a long, hard, and dangerous task. At the time, there were not yet any horses on the plains, and the Native Americans had to stalk and capture the buffalo on foot.

The hunters were always in danger of being trampled.

In those days, the Cheyenne relied on dogs to pull their *travois* (trav-WAH). These were primitive wagons fashioned from poles, used to carry home the buffalo meat and the hides.

The buffalo was very valuable to the Native Americans of the Great Plains. This animal provided them with just about everything they needed to live. When the meat of the buffalo was dried and mixed with marrow and fruit, it became food that would keep for long periods of time.

From the hides of the buffalo, the Cheyenne and members of other tribes made ropes, shields, and clothing. Eventually the Native Americans used buffalo hide to make themselves a new kind of house, the *tipi* (tee-PEE). Buffalo sinew, or muscle, was used to make bowstrings, moccasins, and bags to carry belongings.

The Cheyenne and the other tribes even found a use for buffalo bones and horns. The bones were used to make hoes to farm the land, and to make runners for dogsleds. Buffalo horns were made into practical household utensils, such as spoons, cups, and bowls.

The Horse Arrives on the Plains

Horses were first introduced to the New World by Spanish explorers, who brought them to Peru in 1519. By the beginning of the next century, large herds of horses roamed the pampas of Argentina. These animals gradually moved northward and westward. By the mid-1700s, all the Native American tribes of the Great Plains had acquired herds of horses.

The lifestyle of the Cheyenne changed in two significant ways after horses came to the plains: The Cheyenne became a nation of skilled buffalo hunters rather than farmers, and they became mighty warriors. The Cheyenne no longer were a peaceful tribe.

With the help of horses, the Cheyenne were able to pursue the prized buffalo and other game more efficiently than before. On horseback, they could surround, capture, and kill their prey more easily and swiftly. The speed of the horse allowed the hunters to travel greater distances to search out the choicest buffalo herds.

Horses, instead of dogs, now pulled the travois. Because the horses were stronger, much heavier loads of buffalo meat and hides could be carried back to the Cheyenne camps.

Within fifty years of the arrival of the horse, the Cheyenne gave up their sedentary lifestyle, and became a nomadic tribe of buffalo hunters. This meant that they no longer stayed in one place, but followed the buffalo herds across the expanses of the Great Plains.

In the mid-1700s, the Sioux introduced the Cheyenne to the tipi. Unlike the earth huts that the tribe members lived in during their days as farmers, these funnel-shaped structures could be transported from place to place. Horses were strong enough to drag large tipis behind them, which meant that the hunters could travel with their wives and children. The Cheyenne became a people constantly on the move.

The arrival of the horse also marked the end of the days in which the Cheyenne were considered a peacemaking people. Horses were such valuable possessions that many plains tribes, including the Cheyenne, often invaded the territory of another tribe in order to raid its horse herds.

The Cheyenne were particularly fond of stealing horses from the Apache and the Comanche, whose large herds thundered across the Great Plains. This horse pilfering sparked many battles between tribes, and created bad feelings that were to last for many generations. Nonetheless, it became an act of great bravery to steal a horse from an enemy's camp. In addition, horses belonging to the enemy became an important part of a tribe's reward for winning a battle.

Another cause of warfare between the tribes of the Great Plains was competition for control of the territories richest in buffalo. This competition heated up after the arrival of the horse. As hunters traveled greater distances in pursuit of buffalo, they often trespassed on hunting grounds claimed by other tribes. The Cheyenne constantly battled a number of tribes for control of good hunting lands.

Not only did the horse create new reasons for fighting, but it also changed the nature of warfare between the tribes. The horse enhanced the stature — and status — of warriors, who could now fight their enemies on horseback, splendidly dressed in colorful war costumes. Horses also made it easier for warriors to count *coup* (koo), a custom of war that entailed touching the enemy's body during the course of battle.

Law and Order

According to tribal legend, a prophet named Sweet Medicine came to the Cheyenne many centuries ago. Before his arrival, there was chaos among the members of the tribe. But Sweet Medicine brought law and order, and is credited with setting up the tribe's governing body, the Council of Forty-Four.

The Council convened once every year, during the summer. At this time, the ten bands of the Cheyenne tribe gathered together to hunt and perform certain tribal ceremonies. The Council was made up of forty-four chiefs who served for ten years. Four of the chiefs were elected from each of the tribe's bands, and four chiefs were chosen from the previous decade's Council.

Each annual session of the Council of Forty-Four was held in a specially constructed Council lodge. Here the chiefs discussed issues and problems within their tribe, and made decisions about their dealings with other tribes.

The Council's head chief, called the Sweet Medicine Chief, performed political and religious duties. He was the keeper of the Chief's Medicine, a sacred bundle of grass that was brought to the tribe by Sweet Medicine.

The chiefs of the Council had great power, but this power was shared amongst them. They did not have one chief who had absolute authority, which confused and frustrated the early white travelers to the Great Plains. Settlers and officials of the U.S. government wanted to deal with a single individual who had

the power to speak for, and sign treaties for, the entire tribe. This was not possible within the existing structure of the Cheyenne government.

In addition to this governing body, Sweet Medicine also established a code of behavior by which all chiefs and tribe members were to live. The standards set for the Council chiefs were particularly high. A chief was expected to be brave, kind, and selfless. Above all, he was to be a peacemaker. This meant that he had to be courteous and generous to all strangers — even if they were his enemies.

Sweet Medicine taught the Cheyenne that if a stranger appeared at their tipis and asked for something, the stranger's request must be granted. These teachings have lasted for hundreds of years. Today, the Cheyenne tell the tale of a

twentieth-century chief, Medicine Bear, who came across a poor Arapaho Indian who was wandering along the road. Acting in the spirit of Sweet Medicine's teachings, Medicine Bear jumped off his horse and gave it to the Arapaho.

The laws of Sweet Medicine also governed the behavior of the rest of the Cheyenne tribe. The people were instructed not to take anything by force or without permission. There were forbidden to say anything bad about members of other tribes — especially the leaders. The Cheyenne were also expected to take great pride in their bodies, and to keep them clean and healthy.

It was clear that Sweet Medicine had very high expectations of his people. And the Cheyenne took the prophet's words very seriously.

Cheyenne Sun Dance held about 1900.

Religious Ceremony and Sacred Objects

The religious worship of the Cheyenne centered around two revered objects: the Sacred Arrows and the Sacred Medicine Hat.

Legend has it that Sweet Medicine found the Sacred Arrows near Bear Butte, a peak in the Black Hills of South Dakota, and brought them to the Cheyenne. The members of the tribe believed that these arrows had special powers that would help them to hunt buffalo and to triumph over enemies in battle.

One of the Cheyenne's most important tribal ceremonies involved the Sacred Arrows. This ceremony, called the Renewal of the Sacred Arrows, was performed annually on the longest day of the year, when the tribe's bands gathered together.

The tipis were set in a large circle around the Sacred Arrow Lodge. Here priests carried out the ritual, which took four days. The feathers of the arrows were replaced with new ones, and the arrows were tied onto a stick in a certain formation. The men of the tribe — but not the women — were then allowed to view the arrows. At the end of the Renewal, anyone who had taken part in the ceremony was expected to participate in a purification ritual.

The Cheyenne's second sacred object, the Sacred Medicine Hat, was given to

Cheyenne drummers at Sun Dance, 1890s.

the tribe by the Suhtai, who became part of the Cheyenne. The Hat was placed in a bag made of buffalo hide, along with five scalps from enemy tribes.

Also kept with the Hat was the Turner, a piece of leather with fringe made of hair. The Cheyenne warriors believed that this object had the power to protect them from an enemy's bullets during battle. The Hat bundle was opened only on very special occasions, and only with great ceremony.

The Sacred Arrows and the Sacred Hat still exist today. The Northern Cheyenne in Montana had possession of the Sacred Hat. The Sacred Arrows have been with the Southern Cheyenne in Oklahoma since 1877. The two objects are kept in

special tipis, under the care of a Keeper, an individual chosen to look after them.

Of all the Cheyenne's tribal rituals, by far the most important was the Sun Dance, performed by many of the tribes of the plains. The dance is an ancient custom that allegedly began during a time of terrible famine. The Cheyenne were told that conducting a tribal dance would regenerate the earth and end the tribe's troubles.

The Sun Dance was held each summer at the coming together of the tribe. The principals in the dance were the Sun Dance Maker, the individual who agreed to sponsor the dance as an offering; and his wife, or a woman chosen to help him. Also participating in the dance were the priests; former Sun Dance Makers who acted as instructors to the Sun Dance Maker; and warrior dancers and their instructors.

The entire ceremony went on for eight days. During the first four days, the Sun Dance Maker and his wife were isolated in a special tipi with the tribal priests. Meanwhile, the rest of the tribe constructed the Sun Dance Lodge, a round structure centered around a tall pole. It was here that the dancers conducted the second half of the ceremony. For four days and four nights, warriors performed a dance consisting of many steps, as well as songs, prayers, and offerings.

Finally, the warriors ended the ceremony with a rather gruesome ritual. Rawhide ropes attached to their chests were tied to the center pole. The warriors would then dance until they bled, torturing themselves because they believed that it would guarantee that their prayers would be answered. The warriors also thought that this ritual proved their bravery and their ability to withstand pain.

Cheyenne Society

The Cheyenne led structured and orderly lives. The roles of men and of women were clearly defined, and social and cultural mores were closely observed.

The men of the tribe were responsible mainly for hunting and for protecting their territory and horses from enemies. It was very important for a young Cheyenne man to prove his courage and develop war skills at a relatively early age. His accomplishments in this area gained him great respect within the tribe. A man's chances for being elected a chief were greatly increased if he had proven himself to be a courageous warrior.

The development of war skills was also very important to the Cheyenne. The tribe was organized into five military societies: Bowstring, Dog, Elk, Fox, and Shield. Each society had four leaders, and each group had its own war dress, rituals, and chants.

The military societies gathered regularly to hold feasts and to perform dances in celebration of their battle feats. These dances also had a social purpose, as they were often used by young warriors to impress young women. The women would often sing their own songs in response, to encourage the warriors. It was very important for a young Cheyenne to establish his bravery and military prowess before he began courting a woman.

As for women, the Cheyenne considered purity and modesty to be important virtues in a woman. Courting couples had to follow strict rules. A young man did not ask for a woman's hand in marriage by himself, but instead asked one of his elder relatives to approach the family of his beloved with his proposal.

After the bride's family consented to the match, the bride-to-be was escorted to the home of the groom, whose family prepared her for the ceremony. The marriage was followed by a festive celebration. The bride and groom were given a tipi of their own, which was located near the tipi of the bride's family.

Caring for the home and raising the children were the key responsibilities of Cheyenne women. Using grass, earth, and buffalo hides, they made furnishings for their tipis. The women transformed these simple structures into comfortable, inviting homes for their families. The women also had the job of packing up the tipi and the family's belongings when the tribe changed camps.

Cheyenne women worked long and hard to keep their husbands and children fed. They gathered and cooked the vegetables, roots, and fruit that were so important to the Cheyenne diet.

When Cheyenne men returned home from the buffalo hunt with their travois filled with hides, the women went to work. Using tools made from buffalo horns, they began the laborious task of cleaning and tanning — or softening — the hides. After the hides became supple and had been dried in the sun, the women made them into clothing and moccasins for their families.

Cheyenne women were extremely inventive. At first, they were able to create beautifully decorated objects using only horsehair, feathers, animal bones, and animal skins. After the white traders and settlers infiltrated the Great Plains in the 1800s, Cheyenne women embellished clothing and crafts with the colorful trinkets and novelties that the new-comers brought. These included beads, cloth, commercial paints, and metal.

The Cheyenne Encounter the White Man

Yellow Wolf, Chieftain of the Southern Cheyenne during the U.S.-Mexican War.

The first white men with whom the Cheyenne had extensive contact were the European and American trappers and traders who came to the plains in the early years of the nineteenth century. For the most part, these white men treated the Cheyenne and other tribes fairly, and the two groups remained on friendly terms for many years.

But along with the new and welcome goods, foods, and weapons that the white traders introduced into the lives of the Cheyenne came things that were much less appealing. Among these were many diseases that the Native Americans had never encountered and, therefore, had no immunity against. Smallpox, cholera, and measles spread through Cheyenne communities, causing many deaths.

The white man also introduced the Cheyenne to whiskey, which led to the downfall of many tribesmen. The traders were known to ply the tribesman with alcohol, for which they had no tolerance. They would then trick the drunk natives into trading away their valuable possessions, such as horses, weapons, and clothing. There are accounts of senseless outbreaks of violence in Cheyenne villages, caused by tribesmen drinking too much whiskey. Unfortunately, alcoholism became a serious problem among the Cheyenne during the nineteenth century.

In 1828, two traders from Missouri, Charles and William Bent, formally set up trade relations with Yellow Wolf, a Cheyenne chief. The Bents built a trading post in southern Colorado. Known as Bent's Fort, the post was among the first permanent structures established in Cheyenne territory. It meant that the white man had come to the Great Plains and was planning to stay.

It was also in the 1820s that the Cheyenne first encountered representatives of the U.S. government. In July, 1825, General Henry Atkinson and several Cheyenne chiefs signed what was to be the first of many treaties between the tribe and the U.S. government. Atkinson had been instructed to travel up the Missouri River to make peace with as many Native American tribes as he could.

The signing of the treaty took place at the mouth of the Teton River in South Dakota. Known as the Friendship Treaty of 1825, this pact was meant to declare friendship between the U.S. government and the Cheyenne. It also had provisions that regulated commerce and secured the safety of white traders and settlers traveling through Cheyenne lands. This treaty helped to create peace between the tribe and the white man, but it was a fragile peace that was painfully shattered by the middle of the century.

Trouble with Other Tribes

At the time the Cheyenne were starting to trade with the white man, the tribe was growing larger and stronger. The Cheyenne acquired new friends as well as new enemies among the other tribes of the Great Plains. They made alliances with the Sioux and the Arapaho tribes, who often supported the Cheyenne in their wars with enemy tribes, including the Pawnee, the Comanche, the Crow, and the Apache.

One significant battle, in which the Cheyenne joined with the Arapaho to attack an encampment of Comanche and Kiowa, took place in 1838. As was often the case, the cause of this clash was horse thievery.

The Cheyenne had sent a party to steal horses from the Kiowa. With the help of the Comanche, the Kiowa captured and scalped the members of the expedition. The Cheyenne and the Arapaho then retaliated with an attack on a village in Oklahoma that was occupied by Comanche and Kiowa people. Before retreating, they killed many of the villagers, including women and children. This is known as the Battle of Wolf Creek.

In an attempt to try to halt these wars between the tribes of the plains, a peace council was held at Bent's Fort in 1840. At this gathering, members of the Cheyenne, Arapaho, Kiowa, and Comanche tribes exchanged gifts and signed a friendship pact.

The Treaty of Fort Laramie

As more and more white traders and settlers streamed across the Great Plains in the 1840s, it became increasingly important for the U.S. government to keep on good terms with the Native Americans in this territory. Good relationships with the plains tribes not only made trading easier, but also guaranteed safe passage for the many white travelers crossing the plains.

During the first half of the nineteenth century, a number of treaties were made between the U.S. government and the Native Americans. One of the most important was the Treaty of Fort Laramie, which was signed at a peace council held in eastern Wyoming in September 1851.

The council was a large and grand event. Both the Northern and the Southern Cheyenne, who by this time had become two distinct groups, attended

the gathering . Also present were numerous plains tribes that had been enemies for many years. The council included Arapahoes, Crows, Shoshonis, Sioux, Assiniboins, Arikaras, and Atsinas. Dressed in their striking battle dress, the warriors of the tribes were joined by some 12,000 villagers.

Thomas Fitzpatrick, an Indian Agent for the government, offered the Native Americans gifts of clothing, flour, sugar, and coffee. There was much dancing, singing, and feasting.

According to the terms of the treaty, the U.S. government was to give the plains tribes annuities, specified amounts of money that would be paid each year. In return, the tribes agreed that the government could build roads and military posts in their territories. The tribes also promised to end warfare among themselves and to cease their attacks on white settlers. In addition, the treaty defined clearly the boundaries of each tribe's territory.

The 1850s:
A Time of Tension

The plains tribes who signed the Treaty of Fort Laramie did so in good faith. They did not know at the time that the pact paved the way for many undesirable changes in their lifestyle.

In the years following the peace council, great numbers of white settlers entered the territories occupied by the Cheyenne and the other tribes of the Great Plains. In many cases, these settlers did not arrive in the spirit of friendship that the treaty had proposed.

The white men were often hostile to the Native Americans, who resented the intrusion on their lands. And the white men committed the unpardonable sin of slaughtering many buffalo and other animals on the plains, destroying the Native Americans' hunting grounds.

Understandably, relations between the U.S. government and the plains tribes became very strained. There were a number of clashes between the Cheyenne and small bands of army troops. The Cheyenne also staged several raids on wagon trains of white settlers.

As a result of these incidents, the government sent Colonel E. V. Sumner to confront the Southern Cheyenne in June 1857. Sumner's mission was to teach the tribe a lesson and to let them know that such behavior would not be tolerated.

Knowing that Sumner and his troops were on their way, the Cheyenne prepared for the fight with traditional ceremonies. Ice, one of the great Cheyenne medicine men, told the warriors that the had used his special powers to insure the warriors' safety. He guaranteed that the bullets shot from the enemy's guns would be harmless.

The Cheyenne rode to the battlefield, confident that victory would be theirs. But when they met the federal troops on the plains of Kansas, Sumner surprised the 300 mounted Cheyenne warriors by using sabers instead of guns. Ice's powers were useless against the swords, and the army troops defeated the Cheyenne. A peace treaty was signed between the military and the tribe several months later. But, like many other pacts, this one did not last.

The discovery of gold in the foothills of Colorado in 1858 greatly increased the tensions between the plains tribes and the white men. Driven by greed and the hope of getting rich fast, prospectors invaded the plains in a great "rush." An estimated 80,000 people poured into the area over the next three years. Close behind the prospectors came real-estate developers and settlers. Soon towns sprang up where not too long ago only buffalo had freely roamed.

Within a decade, railroads made their way through territory that was once the hunting grounds of the Cheyenne and other tribes. With the railroad came many more travelers and settlers, further hastening the end of the way of life that the plains natives had known. But it became clear that they were not going to give it up without a fight.

A Crippling Blow: The Sand Creek Massacre

With the loss of much of their hunting territory and the loss of many warriors in battles with U.S. government troops, the Cheyenne were resentful and greatly disheartened. In desperation, the Southern Cheyenne signed a treaty with the government in September 1860. In return for food and clothing, the Cheyenne agreed to settle on a reservation in Kansas.

Many members of the Southern group were disgruntled at the terms of the treaty, which denied them their nomadic, buffalo-hunting lifestyle. Worse yet, the land they were given was dry and unsuitable for farming. This unpopular treaty had additional repercussions. The government later insisted that the pact allowed a railroad to be built through the land assigned to the Cheyenne, who viewed the "iron horse" as another major intrusion on their lives.

Hostilities on the plains heated up in the early 1860s. Members of many tribes, including the Cheyenne, were repeatedly stealing horses and killing the cattle of white settlers.

In the summer of 1864, the government decided something had to be done to end these raids. John Evans, the territorial governor of Colorado, asked friendly tribesmen to travel to government forts for peace talks. Believing that

their bands would be safe if they traveled to Fort Lyon, several Cheyenne chiefs persuaded their people to make the trip.

For one Southern Cheyenne chief and his band, this trust was misplaced and the results were tragic. Chief Black Kettle was directed by the military commander at Fort Lyon to remain in his camp on the Sand Creek River rather than complete the journey to Fort Lyon. The commander assured Black Kettle that he and his band would be safe. But a regiment of 700 volunteer cavalry, commanded by John M. Chivington, surprised the Cheyenne while they slept. The troops attacked the camp, slaughtering men, women, and children.

Chief Black Kettle displayed the American flag as a sign of friendship and even hung out a white flag as a signal that he was willing to surrender. But army troops ignored both flags and continued the savage killings. Hundreds of Cheyenne died in this attack, known as the Sand Creek Massacre.

The 1860s:
A Decade of Defeats

The Cheyenne felt betrayed and enraged by the Sand Creek Massacre and were determined to avenge the barbarous assault. Over the next few years, the Great Plains became an often-bloody battleground. The Cheyenne, as well as bands from the Arapaho, Comanche, and Kiowa tribes, staged attacks on wagon trains and white settlements throughout the Kansas and Colorado territories.

As a result of these frequent raids, sentiment grew against the Native Americans. The U.S. government called several peace councils where short-lived treaties were signed with the Cheyenne and other tribes.

As the 1860s came to an end, two key losses on the battlefields were particularly crushing to the Cheyenne. In November 1868, Lieutenant Colonel George Armstrong Custer was on an expedition in Oklahoma in search of bands of Cheyenne. He came upon a group of the tribesmen led by Chief Black Kettle. The band was camped peacefully by the Washita River. In an unprovoked, surprise attack, Custer and his troops descended on the Cheyenne village, slaying many of the tribe, including Black Kettle.

In July 1869, the fiercest of the Cheyenne military societies, the once mighty Dog Soldiers, received a fatal blow. Led by Chief Tall Bull, the Dog Soldiers were camped near the Platte River in Kansas when they were attacked by U.S. Army troops, commanded by Major E. A. Carr. The Cheyenne camp was wiped out. After this battle, the Dog Soldiers were never again a threat to the U.S. government.

Some of the surviving Dog Soldiers went to live in Sioux villages. Others, in desperate need of food and housing, went to the U.S. government for help. Although there were still isolated bands of Cheyenne roaming the Great Plains, the tribe no longer controlled the lands that had once been theirs. By 1870, the Cheyenne had become a scattered, powerless, defeated people.

(Photo courtesy of Colorado Historical Society)

Sand Creek, from a painting by Robert Lindmeux.

19

Resisting the Reservations

Signed in 1867, the Treaty of Medicine Lodge was one of the many pacts made between the U.S. government and the plains tribes in the 1860s. It designated a barely habitable section of Oklahoma as a reservation for the Cheyenne and the Arapaho. Brinton Darlington, who was appointed Indian Agent to the Cheyenne, moved the reservation farther south, into more desirable territory. This territory became known as the Darlington Agency.

Darlington, a Quaker, felt that the Cheyenne were capable of living peacefully on a reservation. But he had certain ideas about how the Cheyenne on the Agency should live, and these ideas were not acceptable to all the members of the tribe.

Darlington was determined to set up

ment troops under the command of General Philip H. Sheridan attacked many settlements of the Southern Cheyenne throughout the Plains. The army soldiers stole horses, ammunition, and food from the Cheyenne.

By the beginning of 1875, most of the Southern bands that still roamed the plains were destitute and gave up the fight. Homeless and hungry, they took refuge on the Darlington Agency.

Throughout the 1860s, the Northern Cheyenne, under Chief Little Wolf and Chief Dull Knife, had continued to resist the government's attempts to place them on the Darlington Agency with their Southern brothers. These Northern Cheyenne felt strongly that they belonged in the northern hills, not on the Oklahoma plains. Their anger at the large numbers of prospectors and settlers who flooded their lands reached a peak in 1866, when the government built three forts on territory that the Northern Cheyenne still considered theirs.

Some bands of Northern Cheyenne joined up with Red Cloud, a Sioux chief, to attack repeatedly the forts and governments troops in the area. The combined efforts of the two tribes were largely responsible for the Fetterman Massacre. In this incident, an entire regiment of soldiers, under the command of Lieutenant W. J. Fetterman, was wiped out by the Sioux and the Northern Cheyenne, who lured the government troops into a trap.

The fighting spirit of the Northern Cheyenne was still very much alive, but the momentum of white society's westward expansion picked up speed during the 1870s. The frontier was closing in on the Northern Cheyenne with great force — a force against which the plains tribes were powerless.

schools to educate the Cheyenne children. He also planted crops on the reservation, in hopes of once again making farmers out of the tribesmen. The bulk of the Cheyenne, who had never experienced formal schooling and still longed for the nomadic life of the buffalo hunter, resisted Darlington's attempts to change their traditions and their lifestyle.

Many bands of the tribe refused to live on the Agency lands and continued to roam the Plains. Though small in number and weakened by hunger and disease, these bands could not accept the ever-growing presence of white men on the plains. During the early 1870s, Northern and Southern Cheyenne warriors, as well as members of other tribes, made repeated attacks on homesteaders, wagon trains, and government troops.

In retaliation for these affronts, the military staged an extensive campaign against the Cheyenne. In 1874, govern-

A Fleeting Victory: The Defeat of Custer

The discovery of gold in the Black Hills of South Dakota in 1874 meant further trouble for the Northern Cheyenne. Greed for gold brought hordes of prospectors into the hills, which had long been the home of the Cheyenne, the Sioux, and the Arapaho. According to the Treaty of 1868, a large area of the Black Hills had been given to the Sioux, and the tribe was not about to let the unwelcome miners destroy the land.

Nor did the Sioux want the government to have this valuable territory. Authorities in Washington offered to buy the Black Hills for a small sum, but the tribesmen refused to sell. The government was not happy with this decision and issued orders for those Native Americans who were not yet living on reservations to report to the agencies. Some bands of Sioux and Cheyenne obeyed, but others ignored this command.

Government officials, determined to punish the uncooperative bands, sent three generals with large armies to confront the Sioux and Cheyenne. In June 1876, the army received a stunning blow from warriors led by the great Sioux chiefs, Crazy Horse and Sitting Bull. Commanding three thousand Sioux and Cheyenne warriors, the two chiefs defeated government troops under General George Crook in a battle near the Rosebud River in Montana. The skirmish, known as the Battle of the Rosebud, let the U.S. Army know that Crazy Hose and Sitting Bull were forces to be reckoned with.

These two chiefs led their people westward into the Valley of the Little Big Horn, where they set up a large camp of sixteen thousand Sioux, Cheyenne, and Arapaho. Meanwhile, the U.S. Army was plotting to avenge Crook's defeat.

General Alfred Terry and his troops met with Custer. Custer was still in command of the Seventh Calvary, which had destroyed Chief Black Kettle's village on the Washita River in 1868. Custer's orders were to follow an Indian trail along the Rosebud River, and to wait for additional troops if he came upon an Indian encampment.

The trail led Custer and his men to the camp of Crazy Horse and Sitting Bull on the Little Big Horn River. Custer made two big mistakes: He greatly underestimated the size of the forces led by Crazy Horse and Sitting Bull, and he was so impatient to fight that he did not wait for help from Terry's army.

On June 25, 1876, Custer led an unsuccessful attack against the determined warriors. The Battle of Little Big Horn, which marked Custer's "last stand," lasted less than an hour. The defeated Custer was killed, along with virtually every one of his soldiers.

Cheyenne delegation to the annual meeting of The Nations of Indian Territory, 1875. The man in the background is an interpreter.

Roman Nose, Cheyenne chief.

The Last Years on the Plains

The defeat of Custer at Little Big Horn was an empty victory for the Sioux and their Cheyenne allies. It was no more than a last moment of triumph for these once-powerful tribes of the Great Plains.

The U.S. Army was quick to avenge its loss; troops were dispersed to stamp out the remaining bands of the plains tribes responsible for Custer's downfall. In November 1876, a group of Northern Cheyenne camped by the Powder River in Wyoming was attacked by government soldiers led by General Ranald S. Mackenzie. The village was destroyed and it was not long before the Cheyenne survivors, including their leaders, Chief Dull

Little Wolf, Cheyenne chief.

(Photo courtesy of Oklahoma Historical Society)

Knife and Chief Little Wolf, gave themselves up.

In 1877, the government sent these Northern Cheyenne to Oklahoma to live with their Southern brothers on the Darlington Agency. But the weather was more humid there than in the northern hills, which brought much sickness to the bands that had come from the north. Determined to return home to more familiar territory, a band of Northern Cheyenne escaped from the reservation in the fall of 1878.

Government troops made several unsuccessful attempts to capture the band, which eventually separated into two groups. Led by Chief Little Wolf, the first group made its way to Montana, where it surrendered to U.S. officials and was allowed to settle in what is today the Northern Cheyenne Reservation.

The second group, led by Chief Dull Knife, traveled to the Red Cloud Agency in Nebraska, where the group was treated as prisoners. By the beginning of 1879, their living conditions were so bad that the Northern Cheyenne could stand it no longer. They tried to escape, but many were killed or captured by government soldiers. Eventually, the survivors were sent to join Little Wolf's group in Montana.

During the next decade, the Southern Cheyenne in Oklahoma became more and more despondent as the government tried to force farming and cattle herding on them. The development of the Great Plains had destroyed most of the buffalo herds, and the days of hunting on the plains had come to an end. It was a dismal time for the Cheyenne, relegated to their northern and southern reservations. But the darkest hour was yet to come.

Old Two Moons, leader of the Custer Massacre.

Medicine Bear.

Cheyenne mother and papoose.

The Allotment Act Brings Trying Times

The Cheyenne tried hard to retain their sense of unity and tribal traditions after they had lost their homelands to the white settlers. It was not easy, and the Allotment Act, passed by the government in 1887, made it even more difficult.

The Allotment Act robbed the Cheyenne and other tribes of the only territory they had left — their reservations. The Cheyenne had originally been told that these lands would be theirs forever, but the Allotment Act stated that parts of each reservation were to be broken up into small farms. These would be given to individual Cheyenne tribesmen. The lands that were left over after this allotment would be purchased from the tribes by the government — for very small sums of money. The land would then be sold to white settlers.

The U.S. government insisted this law was good for the Cheyenne, as it would give them their own parcels of land to farm. Many white men who supported the legislation declared it would "civilize" the natives. But owning their own farms meant very little to the Cheyenne and the other tribes of the plains, who had no use for farming.

Instead of aiding the plight of the Cheyenne, the Allotment Act managed even further to fragment tribes that were already broken apart.

The law did make the U.S. government and numerous white real-estate developers very rich. Ninety million acres that had been reservation lands was put up for sale. This meant that many white homesteaders could buy their own piece of the plains.

The Southern Cheyenne endured an additional affront in March 1891. The U.S. government passed a law that opened up to white settlers the tribe's reservation land in Oklahoma, where the Darlington Agency had been established.

With much of their land and many of their treasured traditions gone, the Cheyenne and other plains tribes found comfort in a new religious cult in the late 1880s and early 1890s. This religion, called the Ghost Dance, was brought to the plains tribes by a Paiute Indian named Wovoka. He convinced the plains tribes that dancing the Ghost Dance would help them in their time of trouble.

The Cheyenne and other plains tribes believed that this religion would bring back their lands and the buffalo and rid them of the white man. But belief in the Ghost Dance did not last very long. The Native Americans soon realized that the dance could not restore the old days when they had ruled the plains. Those days were gone forever.

Cheyenne chiefs: Woman Heart, Yellow Bull, Prairie Chief, Red Bird Wolf Chief, Kais, Bear Bow, Thunder Bull, Coyote.

The Cheyenne in the Twentieth Century

Like the other plains tribes, the Cheyenne have faced many hardships in this century. They have often felt betrayed by the U.S. government, which they felt was working against them rather than trying to help them.

Many tribesmen saw the U.S. Bureau of Indian Affairs, which had been set up to manage the tribes, as a mixed blessing. The Bureau changed many of the practices and traditions that had been at the heart of Native American society. Children were sent to schools, where they learned to speak English, and were taught that the right way to live was the white man's way. There was no room in the government-directed formal schools for the traditions that the Cheyenne children's parents and grandparents had passed on to them.

The Indian Reorganization Act of 1934 brought some positive changes into the lives of the Cheyenne and other tribes. It partially reversed the unpopular Allotment Act by putting an end to the distribution of tribal lands to individuals. In addition, the law stated that lands that had not yet been sold to white homesteaders would be returned to the tribes that had originally held them.

But his act also brought political changes to the Cheyenne — changes that further reduced the stature of the tribe's chiefs, whose power had been whittled away since the 1890s. The new law abolished the Council of Forty-Four, the traditional governing body of the Cheyenne. In its place, a new Tribal Council, supervised by The Bureau of Indian Affairs, was formed. The elected members of this council had the authority to make the decisions once made by the chiefs and by the leaders of the Cheyenne warrior societies.

Today, the Northern and Southern Cheyenne are still two distinct groups.

At the beginning of the twentieth century, the Northern Cheyenne began farming their reservation lands in Montana. They grew crops that enabled the tribe to feed itself. In addition, they developed horse-breeding and cattle-herding businesses. Unfortunately, both of these endeavors were hurt by government interference during the first two decades of the century.

In the 1960s, coal was discovered on the Northern Cheyenne's reservation. This had both good and bad consequences for the Cheyenne. The government and large mining companies were determined to get at the coal, even if it meant destroying the land. As they had many times before, the Cheyenne found their territories overrun by greedy outsiders. But at the same time, coal is a very valuable mineral, and its discovery on their land brought the Northern Cheyenne financial compensation.

The Southern Cheyenne have not been as fortunate as their Northern brethren.

Many have left the Oklahoma reservation in search of jobs and a higher standard of living, but lack of education and prejudice against Native Americans have often made it difficult or impossible for them to find jobs with decent wages.

As a result, many of the Southern Cheyenne still live in poverty. The tribe is making gains in improving its situation, but life is not easy for many Southern Cheyenne.

Today, Northern and Southern Cheyenne, like many of the tribes that once reigned over all of North America, are caught between two very different cultures. It is difficult for them to hold on to tribal traditions and rituals while living in fast-moving twentieth-century society.

Yet the Cheyenne have done an admirable job of preserving the tribe's rich and colorful past, while making significant contributions to contemporary American society. It is hoped that these Native Americans will continue to do both as the United States moves toward a new century.

The Bear Above and his wife.

Important Dates in Cheyenne History

1519   Spanish Explorers bring horses to the New World.

1600s   The Cheyenne migrate westward from an area north and west of the Great Lakes into North Dakota at the end of the century.

1700s   The Cheyenne move further westward to the Great Plains, and build villages on the banks of the Missouri River.

1740s   The Cheyenne acquire horses and begin changing from a nation of farmers to a nation of nomadic buffalo hunters.

1825   The Friendship Treaty is signed between the U.S. government and the Cheyenne, in an attempt to create peace between the tribe and the white settlers. The Southern and Northern Cheyenne become two distinct groups.

1828   The first trading post is built in Cheyenne territory, symbolizing the permanent presence of the white man.

1838   A band of Cheyenne and Arapaho warriors defeat a Comanche-Kiowa group in the Battle of Wolf Creek.

1851   An enormous peace council, held at Fort Laramie in Wyoming, brings together the Cheyenne and many other tribes. They sign the Treaty of Fort Laramie with the U.S. government. The treaty gives Native Americans annuities in return for the right to build roads and military posts in their territory.

1857   Government troops under Colonel E. V. Sumner defeat the Cheyenne on the plains of Kansas.

1858   Gold is discovered in Colorado, bringing many white prospectors and settlers to the plains.

1860   Hungry and homeless, the Southern Cheyenne sign a treaty with the government and agree to settle on a reservation in Kansas.

1864   In the Sand Creek Massacre, government cavalry under John M. Chivington stage a savage attack on Chief Black Kettle and his band, who were on their way to Fort Lyon for peace talks.

1867   The Treaty of Medicine Lodge, signed between the government and the plains tribes, leads to the foundation of the Darlington Agency.

1868   Camped by the Washita River, Black Kettle suffers another surprise attack led by Lieutenant Colonel George Armstrong Custer.

1869   Led by Chief Tall Bull, the Cheyenne Dog Soldiers are wiped out in Kansas by government troops under E. A. Carr.

1874   The discovery of gold in the Black Hills of South Dakota means hordes of prospectors invade the home of the Northern Cheyenne.

1876   The Cheyenne join with Sioux warriors under Chiefs Crazy Horse and Sitting Bull to defeat General George Crook in the Battle of the Rosebud. Custer is then defeated at the Battle of Little Big Horn.

INDEX